Whatever it is, gently

Quiet Meditations for the Noise of the Pandemic

By: Devon Spier

Printed in the United States of America

First printing, 2020

ISBN 978-1-7753802-1-4

Author: Devon Spier
Cover Artist: Pauline Williamson
Editor: Hila Ratzabi
Layout and Design: Kevin Romoser

Foreword

these meditations
poured
out of me

like a glass of spilled milk

broken
sticky
smelling

shards
misshapen
bare
a poet's wares!

the following words
and the blank spaces
that encircle them

are dedicated
to those with
brokenness
they dare not fix

oh
the sour sweetness
our worlds wear
in Pandemonia
our hearts
secluded
distanced
dare

(distance dares)

Throughout this book, you will note the name of G-d alternately written as either G-d/g-d/G!d. This is done intentionally both to reflect the millennia-long Jewish custom of avoiding writing the full name of G-d to prevent erasure and also to reflect my personal Jewish practice of understanding the multiple directions of my relationship with G-d. To me, and in each moment, G-d can be many—a still small voice, a lowly diminutive creator being that mirrors my likenesses and, too, my flaws, a lofty sovereign, and an exclamation point of lightning clarity in a peak of powerful and intuitive realization that comes so deep from within me it must be beyond me. But really the point for me and why I choose to use the "-" or other types of punctuation is because as I change, so does G-d, and that in this possible and wholly changing universe and, indeed, pandemic, I am reminded that in my folds, I am unfolding G-d, and that holiness, even in the holes and empty spaces, is unfolding at every turn.

part 1
anger/fear/hurt

you first, dear Heart

on this Page

in this Heart

on this Feed

fear is okay Here

hurt is okay Here

hope is okay Here

relief is okay Here

you are okay Here too

even if you are not okay

we are and can be Here together

thank you for being Here as you are

in this moment

(amen).

hand san
has
landed
in the ball
of my eye

right here
in the middle
of the grocery
store line

i cry and i cry

what the fuck
is with me
not keeping in
line/s

these days

do i really miss lying
when people ask
and i reply

"oh, thanks, i'm fine"

no

but yes

maybe

a little

this is my current state

we are living in the

united states of
pandemonia

in the
beginning

we
felt the
consideration

of
moon
beams

but
for
the glare

of
earth
people

and
their
spotlights ...

whose promise
whose rock
whose time
the water sounds off
but all we hear is tick tock
and the milk and honey has been
delivered to us
store bought

i don't know everything
i will never know everything
i cannot fathom what it is
to behold even a grain of Your Wisdom!

Master of the Universe
tremble my fences
so i am shaken out of the
disbelief that i am alone

create of me the unknowing
to sense my fragments and reject my
certainties embracing the
Sources of Living Life in front of me
The Source Not Me
The UnThirsting Source
You!

my Feeling held
my Fixing close
pointed "Here"
and here
we stayed

whatever it is
gently

where are all the other hearts?
my Lonely Heart wondered out loud

dear Heart

they are
(quiet aching breaking)
all around you

listen
find them
cradle each other
so you can find life
and the words again

tl;dr
don't discount your time or this season

in times of chaos and uncertainty, look out for everyday
wonders, for instance –

if you are reading this you are making it through today

and someone who is having trouble making it through the
day is seeing this and thinking:

"if they can do it, i can make it through this one, too"

sometimes we supply the precise kind of wonder somebody
else needs to find wonder in their own life to rejoice in the
beauty of being alive

we can be unalone as we empty
and we can be undone when we
are just plain done
there are hands hidden wings opening to you in every
back heart flattening fiber of the isolation you're in

(something else

depth
deep
deeper deep
deepest deep
bottom
rock
hard
death?
still deep
and here in the last place you would expect
levity

but first this ...)

grief isn't just death
life isn't just death
and life isn't just life

(feel)

people are in pain
that's the prayer to say
i hear you
i am listening to you
your words
and you
amen
amen

check in
don't shut out
ask
don't assume
look out
not only in

amen

you do not
– have to be positive
– do pirouettes with your sadness
– pretend

it's a pandemic, not a carnival

you can
– let yourself be
– let the people who love you know if you need something
different than what they're offering you

we can
– all afford to take better care of each other, even if it's just
accepting people as they are feeling

elohai neshamah
my g-d of soul
blessed are
you
for leaving traces
of our souls
as our bodies fall
thank you for reminding us
of the hidden breath
the raspy rapt blessing bound up inside us each day
unwavering
that we are alive
when the world
when we least expect to be
we are
amen

love is groceries
and grimaced faces
when milk is spilled
and hearts hit the floor
and tissues that find their way to
waste baskets
the unwonderful
used band aids
and muddled schedules
muffled coughs
stuffed ears
the one hundred and twentieth
bless you
a little trite
exhausted
inexhaustible
uttered on a day that's true

i had these two papers
wrapped around my pockets my whole life
every time i took them out
they got older
and so did i
my yellow heart i thought
no courage
just years
but anyway
a day came
today
and i felt the words paperless coming through
speaking then singing in
my mouth
"the world for your sake"
actually means
for *my* sake
g-d loves me
all of me
anyway
i have always been near to you
and i will bring other people near to me too
g-d of mystery
g-d beyond the words
G-d Who Loves Us Anyway

where you are is not wrong
this is just your heart's song –

fear
fear
fear
fear
fear
fear
screams
listens
softens (and again)

as i urge people
to seek help
may i first and foremost
be a person
who reaches
out for help especially when i feel most helpless

(amen)

g-d
i am giving you/giving up
other people today
so you can free me up to be
who i really am
so i can free you up to be who you
really are too

Sheltering Lord
lay each of us down
so we may be raised up
in life
guard our coming from control
and our going to separate peace
and save us for your name's sake

amen

the thing about beauty is
we don't have to know
and in and out and out and in
miracle
she strolls

how to give your heart away –

1. take your heart back

where do
You dwell
when the world's a mess

wild
wild
wilder
wilderness

how awful is this place
how awe filled is this place
to wrestle wild with G-d awake

"are and have been" are a single body of water to visit
lovingly and often;

so wake us and quake us, seismic ones!

and don't give up a single fragment of who you are for
anyone.

trust that what you bring – you – are just right – at every
moment along your way. You are the movement, the moves,
the way.

and you have the grace and the gall of Rivers.

(you couldn't run dry if you tried).

here's to the addicts
and
the chronically ill

and anyone whose isolation
has no end date

"until..."

y(our) existence
y(our) bodies
and
y(our) very lives

are infinite
truthful
holy
and wise

and the whole world can (re)learn how to live because of
you (us)

we are still making

dear Heart
there are heart songs
your heart
your songs
to be sung

and what if i told you
you have been singing all life long?

the world quiets
at sight of the wound
but
you were born with your HeartMouth open

River birthing G-d through tune!

where they would look away you would have them listen
and see see them listen now and see water to desert You
the music World weeping unwrapped at last and free!

today's prayer
i nestle into
the wall of my home

the wall i share
with yours

in a building
in a town
in a country

not mine
but ours

"how are you really?"

and for a mere second
there is no frantic terror
rebuked horror
or masking pain

we are separate
and unmasked

our love in loneliness time is Eternity

take your fear
turn it up
and around
come in close
soul unbound

hi i'm lonely
but
if you're
lonely
that means
i and we are not alone
where there is no presence
there is Presence
and where there is Presence
care

(care)

i make no use of and have exactly no talent the stories are
telling me and it's my job to listen

routine breaker
holy unmaker!

let your embrace
come in the embraceless embrace between rooms and
screens grocery aisles and streets
and let me the emptied emptying know that through
these heart eyes
oh yes even the anxious averted eyes
you see me
and we are holding feeling
and not once departing the other
in unprecedented time
we are still finding Time
to Love

in this leaving
there is a longing

and in this longing
there is a raging

and in this raging
there is a grieving

and in this grieving
there is an enjoining

and in this enjoining
suddenly
unavoidably but perhaps ever-presently

loving

and in this loving
a living

in crisis time
heed the words

retrieve the Word

Yours
Ours
never mine

the polluted earthen River constantly unwinds
and
unsublime

all i find
is
cursedness
turned to
gift of rhyme

Selah

we have been in the wilderness before

and

we cannot grasp so hard at blooming

that

we neglect to cross our own shores

the sandless waterless shores!

to face away from G-d

is to turn our backs to the grave

oh My Fearful Ones

wail

doubt

wander

this is the Wild

this is the Wave!

49

remember

the stranger

lest your heart

become

a shackle

and a stone

become the surface

of your skin

in solitude

i am overcome

by the wonder of freedom

that

i touch y(our) loneliness

and unalone

at last

i let you

stranger

all the way in!

i thought myself
an undersized aleph

but instructed to be
an oversized aleph

i dressed up my aleph

only to discover
i wasn't reading torah

i had looked but hadn't unwrapped a single word

it was only when my mouth opened
and chest shouted out of me

Bet!

that i knew i wasn't writing heaven or earth
but a present unlocking the future
and beginning without end

abandon all tall tales
and just tell your tales

in your mouths
the silent letter
reviving the long silent g-d
to shudder utter

Holy Speech!

sometimes

when
i have no
words
to pray

i just start
saying people's
names

and
between each
pause i curl up
against

i swear
i hear

g-d's delighted

"yes!"

exclaim

a psalm of no sprung spring –

i never feel so alive
as when i renounce
every dead thing i have
mistaken for life!

i am tremendous
i am towering
i am the tallest tree in the field

i am bent over
i am unbuttoning my shirt
i am bruised
i am bereft of thirst
i have forgotten how to thirst
or maybe i never quite learned how

i am breaking
i am bowing
to the g-d who made me
who exists beyond me
distant and apart

so can i
a voice
amen

now
a generation's long awaited rain
amen

i am human once again!
amen

for what feels like
the first time
i don't grow

i have my own body
mouth and soul

amen

how do i take care of others when i can barely take care of
myself?

no one
has ever
will ever
remove
a plague
from their house
by casting a
plague
on
their house

the questions
i don't ask g-d –

how many tens
how many hundreds
how many
millions
how many of us
some
seven billion
will it take
to make something
other than death
of life?

Blessed are the nameless

To whom names were given but then silently taken

Blessed are the nameless

Who died by our unknowing of their very lives, worlds and
breaths

as you
make
your bread
can you
surmise
there are
those
of us
trying to
locate
our
mouths
can
you print that
on a recipe card
place at the bottom
of plastic tupper
ware

where?

nothing
is more
distant
than
the

"we
are
in this
together"

hugging
heart
smiley
emoji

in a sea of
click bait
longing
for someone
to sink my teeth
into

so i can sew them back together
again
with the buttons
i keep in my (treasure)
chest

curbside pickup
i have to pee so badly
i have forgotten how
or why
when open is closed
and closed is open
i wonder what else
i've learned
to put down
put off
off put
i don't know about

curse the fire!

and curse the dark!

curse these unlinked arms!

and bottomed out hearts!

and when i am done cursing

permit my being to sink so low

that i surrender

in spite of my solitary hatreds

to

Blessing

to the promise of every last hopeless shred shredding within
me to feel the unfelt dread

and by acceptance let this human life

at last

be led

the world is breaking

they sighed

oh no

the child replied

the world at last is opening

i don't push for g-d
but i do pull g-d
out of places
we'd rather not see
disorder
distrust
misery
the garbage rivers
that are
Our Stream

and i am hopelessly
interested in what
you are really carrying
there

not in your briefcase

some are gone

and some have stayed

but nevermind

i am awake

and this body brays and breaks

breaks and brays

the living language

away

Knower
of Our Hearts

One Who Sets Us
Together Apart

in these days

teach us

make a teaching
of us

as of old –

to be
secluded
but
not alone

distant
but never
to not a single soul
hidden
or
cold

(amen).

i will never
confuse
my need for unrest
with your need that i
rest in peace
ever
ever
again

i am Groundless
i am Blameless
i am Unrepressed

and i am fully
Living

faithfulness
is not naivete

attitude
does not denote
ingratitude

and feeling
does not necessitate
fixing

we are living beings
and we deserve to be alive

to come alive

wherever we find ourselves
breathing or not breathing
each day

(we are still Being)

i found
in the sun
the tiniest
speck

and though
my eye
could not
make out
all the rest

my body knew –

i don't have to do anything

and the word
that builds
in the breadth of my chest?

the
world of fall rise fall and rest?

recreation
the new creation
begins Here

in the sign
in the sigh
in the prayer

let

let

praised be the bearer
of bough and breeze
who gives a single nostril
all the hidden fruits
she needs!

we have been
burning the fires
so long
we didn't notice
our eyes
watering

that we had made the altars
out of our bodies and
lamp shades
out of the invisible sadness
we carry
i think they used to call that
human

can we remember we bled
and go raise the dead
can we borne of flame
and wed to death
live twice
and take flight
without one damned holy act of
sacrifice?

"where are we?"

the flowers of our griefs
have knocked down every door
and moved past every screen

and what of the altars
Edens
and offerings to Paradise?

of religion's loftiest dreams?

seems the gardens are springing
forcibly
fearsomely

but gardens

seeds and weeds
Here are We
planted and free

Kindness is not "Power Over"
Care is not letting
only the powerful choose
And anger is, indeed, a spiritual practice

the third Be-ing

between human and g-d

i never felt it til now

or felt the absence odd

oh but your presence has come
has been a knocking!

and the words so simple this life's unlocking –

"and you shall love you
and when at last you love you
it shall ever be you
you choose"

constriction
is holding our breath
for dear life

and what of a life
that refuses to breathe pain
to experience and corporeally sense

this life is not alive

this life is
ballooning death!

If it's morning where you are, wonderful one, you made it
through the night

And if it's night where you are, you already made it through
the start and end of an uncertain morning

And you are wonderful, too

Wonders in us and beyond us
May they (and we) never pass by Us

ten hidden wonders

– we bleed
– we burn
– we are wild
– we sustain
– we look up
– we experience pain
– we are not the Weathermaker and we have the power to
change the weather
– we grow
– we make light
– we bring life into the world

and longform;

– we bleed: that our lives are shakeable and therefore possible, we are not gods, we are human beings and our present course can be changed as we choose with startling humility that moves us ever beyond ourselves

– we burn: that we have walked and jumped through flame and can pull out the holy and a new way of living when all appearances including our false selves fade away

– we are wild: we can go into the wilderness without becoming the wilderness and we can go back into the world while remaining a bit wild

– we sustain: refusing to let hope fall away and the forces of debased groupthink and lesser hatreds to swarm us and reign

– we look up: to the future, to the horizon, to the world that isn't this and then we go back to the world because we know our work isn't done until we accept and break out of old ways of being and invite in the holy new

– we experience pain: our bodies are imperfect vessels, they bend, break and often, do not make any sense; it is in the senseless that we are implored for be sensitive, to know that the blessing of being human is to be responsible to the other, an imperfect becoming, to become imperfectly

– we are not the Weathermaker and we have the power to change the weather: there is increased awareness of the need to lower our greenhouse gas emissions, which is expected to occur naturally as a result of the current pandemic. and what kind of earth could we will to be if we learned to seek health and justice and to act before the onset

of the latest disaster and disease? what would it mean to move
forward and be more responsible to the earth each day?

— we grow: our isolation does not prolong our collective
loneliness; we can safely text and email our neighbors, we can
send groceries to the stranger down the street, we can knock
down every heart door that uses staying home as an excuse to
hate the worst of our humanity and our own wearying souls;
we can unite alone and act on the very best of us to come
together

— we make light: we start our Jewish days in the dark and
is that not the perfect beginning and ending, exultation and
invitation to being alive?

— we bring life into the world: we find the miracles in the
unlikely places and in time of plagues, we present our lives
to the holy repurpose of making this world more decent and
more whole; yes, even in pointing to the holes; we are Verb
People, a holy People whose words acts and hearts source
out of oppression the glorious gentleness of care, creating
new possibilities for the interlinking of our lives and making
real the promise of freedom overcoming the bondage of fear

you belonged before you boarded the bus this morning

you belonged before you dropped off the kids at their mom's

you belonged before you caught your friend's eyelash resting
lightly atop their eyelid

you belonged before you breathed the lack of air inside the
subway car

you belonged before you got the coffee

you belonged before you pulled into the grocery store

you belonged after you mourned all these things

and when you sit to think of them
someone somewhere is remembering

you belong
we belong to each other
that is how to mop the pieces of our breaking hearts off the floor

no sanitizer
hand or otherwise
required after or before

who said
anything
about
whole

hole
holes
holy
holy day
holidays

it seems
to be
daybreak

the new days
are breaking

so
are we

and we shall be
holy

it was as if our eyelashes
turned to feathers
on angels' wings!

she looked at me
i looked at her
we looked at each other

we had no one
else we'd rather be

i wonder –

when else has g-d stopped into the milk aisle

how else besides not looking
can a human being turn divine

at the end
of all this

will you be able
to reach out to me

like you currently rush to clasp my
credit card

deliberately

what will be the currency
between us

who will pay for the balance owing

tender

Tender

will that mean something different to you to me to the world

what will register

who won't?

daily
my
body
scritch scratches
a poem
a prayer
from the site of her wound

i am changing
Self moves
and I remain

(amen)

today
every day
my doom is my bloom

yes

keep it all together

and once you've bound it all

neatly to your

(their) liking

give the feathers back to the wind

give your body

back to your body

have courage

to be plucked dry

to lay your self bare without so much as a narrowly
averting eye

this is love

to go unnoticed

to carry on is the first limb of flight

a cup of shame
or a cup of praise?

a table for kings
or the path of slaves?

into the burning
our generation's gaze

whose ways?
which way?

and around us
the lowest begs and prays

freedom!

ours
and
Theirs

from watery dry and fiery grave!

and in time
when i feel nothing
in my hand
i will unfold Something
my crumpled up heart

i am redeeming the words
i can hold my own

lord
give me my heart
before i give me
away

permission –
to recast every shackle

this is the drama

this is the dirge

this is the unseasoned season

of our liberation

the drums of war
ring hollow
when met by the sounds
of our bodies

bereft and breached
and left with so little

that all we can talk about
all we can call out from our souls
to the world is

songs of
overflowing
Life

these times are not written
these times are not sealed
these times are wide
wide
open

a human heart beating
back
Truth
against the fury of our fears

get lost from the city
get lost from the show
take a detour your head can't
remember
but your broken back still sows

and when you see that fork hanging there
in the middle of the road

tell us
don't go anywhere –

is there a line
between
shepherd
and
slaughterer

we are here bleeding but we are just too wise to know

the Death angel visited me –

the Death angel

came in quietly
and rested
above my body

and i
words departing me
with only
Shame
(the thief the theft)
consumingly

heard the angel breathing:

"you are not a Living Death..."

and then numbers
out of my mouth
they crept

and the
Life thought a Plague
emerged a Plague
brought to Life

until there was just
One Life
One G-d
nothing
not a fear was
left

to whom i do not concern

i must
impolitely
decline your request
for a song and dance

why do i need you looking
and touching
with your looking

when i am content to
enjoy
to feelingly
feel
my selves
formed
forming?

one must make a living
from Someone other
than some people's controlled longings

my gratitude practice
isn't

– thankfully but deceptively painting over

my gratitude practice
is

– mercilessly and acceptingly paying attention

my body is not the shit someone else says
my body is not the shit someone else says
my body is not the shit someone else says
my body is not the shit someone else says
my body is not the shit someone else says
my body is not the shit someone else says
my body is not the shit someone else says
my body is not the shit someone else says
my body is not the shit someone else says
my body is not the shit someone else says
my body is not the shit someone else says
my body is not the shit someone else says

place/space –

i am changing

the hard place
said to the rock

and the narrowness
crept and wept
between them

until all you could
smell and see
for miles
as a red heart
pumping sea

were cascades of cherry blossoms

there are spaces
we don't know about
until we know
we don't know
we have them

measure/less –

hearts halt
eyes dry out
stomachs lose legs
to stand on

and mouths ache
for words that will not come

and as
the motions appear motionless

making your self
something to eat
is revealed to be
the kindness your soul starvingly seeks

oh
go on
make your soul a
sandwich

oxy/gen –

after
solitude
passes

and
the breath
of
freedom

passes
from your lung
to my
startled
still
opening
face

when the remembrance
of respiration is no mere memory

will we

be swept away
by mind
or government's

fearful gust

or will we change what it means
to feel a human being

will we forget the lies
we traded
for the comfort

of knowing

it is (not) only us
it is (not) only us
it is (not) only us
it is (not) only us

and will we pause then for air
the silent
common prayer

will we listen
below the words
and glares

will our oxygen be
at last
our invocation

bind un/bound –

we are boundless
in our binding
and binding
in our boundlessness

i pray
you are released
from
the burden
of hollow and sleepless prayer
and the penitent whose nightly prostrating
has replaced sleeping
and whose day sleeping has surpassed
their listening

(... G-d? are you speaking? it's me
not g-d...)

i petition for the
release of that which is mine and only mine
so i can come back to bed
come back to the world
and to you
and you
and you
and readied then
at last to
You!

a(part) –

i made a vow
long ago

that i wouldn't let the narrowness i was living in become me

but that was the River of Blood talking

and i was and am the
Sky
listening to the
Universe
above
below

and
oh
yes
now i know

a(part) of me!

I spelled my name wrong today

I am currently waiting, heart-shakingly, to receive a pre-
scription

The cash register rings:

Everywhere
Every/where/here

I am
I am Here

(Amen)

home/stay
meditation –

if
you
can't
stay
out

if you are
tired
of staying in

just for today
say –

your
heart
is
your
home

we are the captive
trying to go free
but a dream
without wilderness
is just the
bottom of the sea

we have to be wild
stuck in the heart
of the wild
to flee!

with/out –

i am
Angry

i don't have to fix being
Angry

i am going to sit with being
Angry

when i want to run out on myself and into the Universe

i am responsible for answering the call within

which is truly the broader echo WithOut

if your life could
speak
these times
what would it/you say?

there is
a word for
prayer
that
lifts up g-d
through
the raising
of a
knife

to whom?

whom
do we offer

this delicious rage
pristine and unplagued
this priestly
not a drop for weeping

banged up
bloody
sacrifice?

to hold alongside your breath in the

checkout aisle
hospital waiting room
not quite vacant
but of course
vacant street corner –

there
was
no
breath
then
the
world

there was
a surface
skimmed
dark
and
moving
and
then
the
world
walked in
eventually

lingering
steps
behind

late

arrived?

we were ended
before we
we began

and now
now
ever
the breathlessness of
the beginning
of life over
disordered
again

when you go to pray
and you look to the heavens above

i want to know

is the god
you are talking to
the shape of a gun?

and around which
center is
your holy book spun?

and of the ink

whose blood?
whose blood?

all we have
to lose is
blood

the unwritten breathless psalm –

from the depths
from the depths
from the depths

they call
to
you

when we order
delivery
when we grab
the last bag of
flour
in the store
we cannot forsake
our story of deliverance
and a world so new it's old
oh the implicit inconveniences of liberation's meandering
way
tonight
maybe
try the self checkout
hop aboard Service's divine train

we made
a
home
there
in the pews

we only lost
everything
above the roof

walls amuse

the walls
are
our muse

oh the
shrinking
expanse
of truth

i uttered
a spell
and
became
undead –

(you cried
"i love you."

i recoiled
"you don't know what love is")

then i turned to love
and
the lead turned to lead!

feel/in/g –

feeling pain is a normal response

i will not let you
let me
outthink
my pain

i don't have anymore
"O, G-d!"

just
oh
g-d

Please

please keep living if you can

please keep learning how to respond so someone who isn't
quite living or doesn't want to keep living can safely land

and please keep sharing the flour

please keep making masks for each other

please keep sending meals to strange houses on strange
streets

please keep donating to fundraisers of people you will
never meet

please keep making forts and wrapping each other in
blankets

please oh please keep taking the time to weep

please keep writing and not writing making art or barely
making due

please keep talking about how illness is not some
politician's war

please keep the bleach from ever touching your window

imaginary or real

please keep noticing how the colors of each day feel

and don't clean that or any of this off
for good

we are trapped
we are under
we are under construction

oh fire
return you
return me
return us
the dead
to the land of the living
so air can be air
life can be life
we will never have to breathe falsely again

we are
informally
invited to
give back
the ignored and impolite
symptoms of
silent raging

the shroud is thickening
our feet bracing
our lungs swallowing
our insides outside
gulping at the masks we tighten to distance
the sense of choking we have come to know as just existing

oh fire
return you
return me
return us
the dead
to the land of the living
so air can be air
life can be life
we will never have to hold to quiet wars mounting

you say the world is enflamed

but
where are the flames
when
we are all drowning
draining away

oh fire
return you
return me
return us
the dead
to the land of the living
so air can be air
life can be life
we can go switching
flip this light switch
to a grievous and watery universe

cross the threshold
open the gates

but this is a prison cell
and these are prison bars!

could you
can you
exist
to me

and still
divine

your mistakes?

(the invisible g-d i have never prayed to admits their mistakes)

Creator
you con
i mean
con cealed
You are
concealed

take my desire
to save face
and meet me
in the moments
i show my own face

and let me show you
who You really are

shame is not love
jealousy is not love
exploitation is not love
celebrity is not love
success is not love

let love be Love!

and let Love love me

i am doing what i can
where i can
however i can
especially when i just can't

and i can be here
just as i am

i don't have to soften
i don't have to sow

i can
not know

and there is still hope

Release from unrelease
Release from forcing release
Release from releasing release
Release from closing ourselves off from release
Release from closing too far in on release
Release

So stay
We are Here
to stay

(There ... release)

part 2
hope/solace/surrender

here we are not

waiting for the appointed
time

we try and try
and
all we seem to have
these days
is the offhand
wrong time

Time as Amos's damned up
waters
damning us and our prearranged pride

still righteousness
rushes and
rages

and unlike us
She will not
cannot hide!

(can we too early
and too late
now
Now
arrive)

found good
found grief
then there was no good

and maybe it was
never good
how could it be

so i lost desire
to find good
then
i felt grief

i don't know
when or if
good will return

but i believe there are pairs
who stop in
to visit us
in our emptiness

and the breadth of life
is
not
has not
will not
cannot be
a cup

every time
the video chat
lags
which nowadays
is always
i tell you the things
i'm not supposed to say

...
...
...

if going back to normal means
going back
to the good sense
not to be delayed
i don't want to be anywhere but
Here

my life
is in
Your hands
but please
never
let
me
forget
my hands

typing trembling trepidatiously
a prayer
that says
nothing

and just catches
the dust of a giggle
the oneness

of a tear

every
time
i say the
krias shema
i end up
hitting
the
backspace
key

sickness has forced down
our throats
the interminable
sometimes terminal
Eternal inquiry

who is a Jew
without
a drop of
pride

i will not make a life
i will not mouth a shred of life
from idols
from snakes or calves' tongues

where can i visit the ancestors
if i abandon the garden
and walk past the field

sweetened people
bittered

a Sanded Down People

we must return
to live in this place
we have never been

remaining apart
to become
departed

then
no pride

Love comes
Inside

morning/mourning –

and perhaps
all the grace
is not locked away
in Graceland

or some kind of guarded kingdom or glorified
Heaven

(and how can one help but feel each one sounds a prison?)

but perhaps
grace is
in the gracelessness of
unspecial hours and days

and each of us
how unremarkable!
who deign to take a breath in the morning knowing full well
we are not g-d

we once were
of course
but that was before
we discovered
the truest mourning
and learned
what it means to get up

give up
locked
unlocked
to live

because
my life
comprises
deaths

i have found
in my one life
many
lives

and first
throughout
concurrent

Death
entering
weighing

but i
i am no longer waiting
i am no longer grabbing hold of
head on

i am
colliding
out of my head
narrowly

Elsewhere

straight into
Life

in
reaching
for our former lives
have we forgotten
to fight for
Life
to feel for
a future
that isn't death?

you were meant to sit
you were meant to cry
you were meant to offer up your gloved hand to perfect
strangers
you were meant to repair and to break to break and then
to repair
you were meant to arrive this day
exactly as you came
you were meant to
draw near to the work of
never-ending staying away

wrap your
arms

'round
your
self

child

and
know how
the fire began

not from
their
wrath

(later ash)

no

from
the touch
of

chemicals
against
the oxygen

(breath)

of your own
soul

i recall
the whirl of the
tea cups

and the laugh
that rang
through us

as we rode
out
ourselves

in the dizzying
circle of the ride

that's why i know

behind every
shut down
shut out door

between every
frenzying
or
humdrum routine

there is a rhythm
and there is a rhyme

the new fair isn't fair

but
in the spinning

i swear i hear

bells ringing
motions praying

a new word
reaching out
for g-d

and a faith
that stains
our teeth

holds to
the roof of
our mouths

surprise

a time
a season
a reason
for
popcorn

here
now
waves
of us
gather
to meet
the tide

to place in
between
my dry mouth
and
watery eyes

when
i crave
the salty
taste
of the
ocean

today i chose a different stop –

we are not Beginning again
because we never left

and yet

we can still

take

the right train
to the wrong station

make history

strange/r

families
were forged
from the breath
of complete strangers

wired wireless and woven

together
a
breathless mess

and families fettered
with familiar
blood
money and births

preordained
all accounted for
no accidents

were found to be
stalled remote
and strange

who is a home
and
are you boxed in
or breaking through
your own rib cage

to land
on the unset table

the altar
of this great emergency

you turn from suffering
and think

"now what?"

what you have
yet to ask
ought to ask

is

"Whom?"

the answer to now is
whom

possibly
the mystery of the
universe
too

g-d
i am changing

you are unchanging

outside
a place
i spasmodically touch

and yet inside
daily
a sentence
is
handed down
to me

a sentence
i can
hands-free
routinely
clutch

i am forgetting everything i learned about grammar
so i thought you
and your invisible gavel
should know

i am changing g-d

every last thing with soul

unstolen
breathing life from
old

with soul

without?
impossible

you tell
you told

that is your soul

every last thing in this life

with your (w)hole(d) soul

g-d

grant me the peace

of knowing

the path to rest

is through unrest

and this gradual

mysterious and grounding

unearthing

you are not a rock
so rock yourself back
and forth
back
but always forth
forth
to the life of an actual human being

blessed are the gate lifters

from the tears of your griefs

a garden we have often dreamed of
gone searching for

but never fully grasped or gleaned

blessed are the gate lifters

whose lives have gone through
great pains to give us the gifts of great

change

who transmit the fragile power
of a single flower in a secret anguished spring

i have grown
tired of staring
at my own face

so i beseech
you

air

go on

touch
my cheek

while i
pretend
to tie my 'lace

what is
a while coming

what is
too
long
gone

when
here we are
dancing to
Eternity's
brand new song?

for days when down is up
and up is upside down –

we have
come to the edge
of grief and loss
and felt our selves
barreling over

and it is still an edge
still a cliff
still a fraction of ground
we are standing on

so
what if we
hell bent and bounded by the earth
terrified at all the fall
felt our backs as wings

suddenly got up
from sitting scared
looked up fell all the way up
and flew?

there is a future
that was born
before we
lost everything

our losses
are impractical
hopes

g-d is remembering –

g-d is trying to remember
we wish g-d would remember

we remember

it is okay
to feel sad today

she told
the little person
gently

and then what at first
was sinking was landing
was stopping was starting
was a hollowing void
is ever an instrument strung out
stringless
and singing

all this melody from one inextirpable sad feeling

and on the eighth or eight hundredth day ...

i can't remember the
night or the day

i am creating
a new act in time

joy in the body g-d has made
joy in the body g-d has made
joy in the body g-d has made
joy in the body g-d has made
joy in the body g-d has made
joy in the body g-d has made
joy in the body g-d has made
joy in the body g-d has made

what
is the use
of this time outside time

of a verse and a life that wind and wind

i lay down my euphony
and force of rhyme

and in
coughs
holiness

which
by the burn
of heart and lung
unsows us unwhole

we don't have to wait until the beginning to begin again

and what is all this nostalgia if
we remember to dream?

delicateness is unfolding splendor here

where is your heart really today?

whom is your heart really today?

with whom is your heart really today?

may
we
not
be
so
reckless

with
our
safety

that
we
fence out
our humanity

and
may
we
separate

from
the
fear

that would promise our
restoration

but entrench only
the
normalization
of racism
stratification
and our political
destitution

and may we
maintain the fences
we need
and remove all the ones
we don't

and may we
never
mistake
staying in
for staying
away

and may we know
home in the places
and people we least expect

and may we reside there
even remotely
but always hopefully
boundlessly
and
often

and may
we always find a window
even if we have to draw one
on the walls

i am living
for the world

in which
lord is displaced from
Lord

in which
Leonard Cohen
does not utter
the last
the final
"hallelujah"

in which
our praise words
break through our bodies
ascend on high

Hallelu

Jah

gasping
past the man
made mountains

Presence
presenting

not a note
performing

new songs singing
lifting the words of G-d
through all the sunken old air/s

back to the open mouth of the universe
awaiting music
awaiting
Us

for the muzzled g-d of repeat
to stop and speak Their own words
really Our words

Hallelujah!

there is
so much

almost

too much
pain to hold

i am giving up
trying

and

cradling
my
Ought's

in

Is

for when there's no end in sight and the poets at this late
hour who write –

you write

one line

i write

another

your line catches hold of mine

my line grabs hold of yours

and someone we

won't ever know

in some place we've never

been or will be

catches their breath

i think we're writing

a lifeline

typo

sorry

laundry line

poems/Poem

i am so out of time
time is all i have

and i am not
(going to be)
okay

but your distant step
striding
closer to me
is dearer
than my same old boring heart
beating

i am tick-ing

and
i have
you have given me
a brand new ticker

and you have successfully
defused the bomb

the explosion everybody knows about
but nobody sees

all because i can hear my heart
in your feet

resolve/d

you have heard
g-d has heard
we have all
heard

the familiar strings of striving pains

(chorus)

benediction
lament
resolution
refrain!

but have you
for the first time
felt the singular
nearness
of your own angel wing?

and
as she
wrote
she
released
every hatred
like
a paper crane
against
an unrepentant
wind

to sing
now

to be

mystery solved
unresolved
and
truly
free

blessed
are you
creator of the universe
who recreates
our days
as nights
and our nights
as days

at the market
today
the sun was shining

and
people were smiling
in public

for what felt to be
the first time
in weeks

so
of course
i welled with tears

heaven knows
there is nothing godlike
about this

human
imposed
season

oh
i guess
that
makes me
normal

i don't think
i will read
the weather
forecast
ever
again

i've been
hitting my head
against this wall
so long
i forgot
i am daisies
pushing
pushed all the way
up
toward a sun that
feels like Death
in a Spring that is straightforwardly
unapologetically
Life

the outside
of my body
is
lined with hurts

but
the inside
of my body
is littered
with hopes

that's why
i believe
any body
is somebody

and when
i say i am looking out
for you

i mean
i am ever
looking in
at you

at all you will be
nestled in all you are
and have always been

humanity
we are
truly
hard to come by

but oh the
flecks of honest
beauty ...

staying in
but not staying
away –

remaining
distant
without
from
the human
heart
being
led
astray

you are just so wonderful
exactly because you feel you aren't

Up and Through
and
Around and In
unrolling Heaven
in the folds
of my
skin

and there are
new songs
ringing
and
redeeming
out the old songs

beating against
the noise
of the same damn
repeat days

it can be different
it can be so different
so we keep singing and sway

when
you are
in the
presence of
greatness

all you feel
is a great gentleness
pass between
you

the breath of life
the one
whose tiny words
breathe great lives into Life

(who could possibly be singular
who could possibly be small)

i wanted out of the circus
so i asked the trepidatious trapeze bar
and then the vertigo swirling rings
how do i stop trying
the air didn't answer me

e

n

d

nights i can't sleep
days i can't awake
sub(par)consciousness

It takes being broken to break a chain

(Amen, amen, amen, amen ...)

Blessed are You
who breaks the chain

the masters'
but especially

our own

and

Blessed are you
The Captive
who lives to free
those still

enchained

and

Blessed are All
who return us our breaking bodies
who restore us our sleeping souls

i will go under
until i am
blue
in the face
of the Sky

and the divine garment
rapts me
as the hand of a wave

urging me against
the wrapping of the world
that would cut off my breathing

i am being folded
beneath Death's curling undertoe

to remember
i am made a Living Being

we are dying
we are shedding
we are protecting
we are changing

i'm immature
im-matur-ity

i am free

religious views –

i don't make reservations
anymore

updated religious views –

that's great because

g-d doesn't take them

"YOU ARE STRONGER"

... than all the advice printed on all the sign posts
in all the world
and
you dear Heart are the sign and the strength
we have all been waiting for!
and no one
can take you
away from
You

you deserve gentleness
at the exact moment
you feel
most unworthy
of it

how do you count to infinity?

answer:

the cleaners and the construction operators, the crisis line,
grocery store and sanitation workers, the nurses, support
workers, pharmacists and doctors, therapists, on-call chaplains
and the carers, yes, each and every carer, that's how ...

i
am
practicing
kindness
because
i
don't
know
how

inside a heart
a day
inside a day
a heart
tick-tock
tick-talk

we are imperfecting

the art of

exhausting

exalting

and there are notes

we are singing to each other

below the noise of the mute button

l-rd
i am trembling

but you

You are moving

(we are too)

when my face
tires of the screen
(don't worry
never your face)
i imagine
we're a family of corgis
and i inexplicably
remember i am
i can be
human again

been so bored of time
out of time
utterly frozen in time

i am alarmed to find myself
drifting into the first easy sleep

in years
decades
near two months
i've been

this century asleep
the clock still broke
restless soul

i am assured of this
one infinitesimal colossal thing –

time is all i ever did
ever will have
again

you are worth more than the
sum of all the things you don't do

not/naught growing –

today i
taught
myself

growing
is
not/naught –

you
who aren't

washing
clothes

filling your mind
filling a cup
never yours

stretching your toes

you who have no limbs to stretch

you
who are just plain stretched
not thin no

No

thick people
all the still shaking real
thick people of the world

thank you
for all you haven't done

or cannot do any longer

you are looking after Life

for those who don't bother hanging on –

i sit in my house
and fear my
hand has turned to rock
that
i will soon become brick
under the weight
of all this sitting ease

but i try
at least once a day
to leave the house for you

my love
my hands

you are singing your songs
to me through the air
and i am catching each one
as a little girl does ribbon held
balloon

we have been here
we are still here

glory to
not
disappear
by the lightness
of our ancestors
rising on

look around
so we don't miss each other

and i will make a new world from the piles of earth that
cradle old ancestors' bones that give footing to the new ancestors' ancestors' ancestors! to us! oh how our generations
do not dare part when we are hanging on by a limb the
ground puts us all back together again but we still wake up
with dry mouth and wonder why our eyes filling with water
feel as thick as red blood can a human life exist without
form yes but what about metaphor the bones crack then a
thud the earth is rising what if we have been resurrecting
the dead playing g-d with our well worded alchemies
this new world isn't quite new no this new world is bound
bound to be old time for a new periodic table

we can be hopeful
and we do not have to pretend

the existence
of our body
is not a loss
to us

the existence
of our body
is the
divine
presence

made
real
in and through
us

(i will not ever disappear)

(i'm not sure i can explain
but)

my heart is open
because it is closed

as long
as we remain
far apart
i cling to
the other soul
g-d gave me

meaning

my extra soul
is visiting your
extra soul
any time you need

mo
(u)
rni
ng
is
br
ea
ki
ng
as
ar
e
we

mo(u)rning
is breaking
as are we

we are as
breaking
is
mo(u)rning

are you
staring at my
mask with all
that face
you're not
wearing?

great
me too

all views past/present/in/between:

and first this ...

my favorite angels are humans
that bend their misshapen bodies and useless good inten-
tions into shelters thicker and daintier than any flappable
wing
span
we are part
apart
i know your holiness
is out there
past your homes
carrying the feather brick
brokennesses
all our hopes on the wind

have no fear

no
have fear

if you don't know
what to make of your
life

your art is your breath

breath-less

you are
creating

Life

a secret recipe
a personal alchemy
to take back to the world
after lockdown
but to practice every day before –

take the platitude or phrase you seriously hate
+
add the word "but"
+
say what you are feeling right now
=
and that's your life verse

aka

the wisdom
you are weaving
with
your luminous
and
numerous
life

be/long/ing –

we don't have
to touch
to gather

we can lead
and be led
unto grief
unto hopelessness
unto shared distance and despair
unto completely unintended
attentive
real live breakable belonging

oh
how
this/be/long
and
we/be/longing

isn't that all the promise
the presence
of longing there is?

something is brewing
in you
yet

you are your own cup
and
all that left

trust the magic
witness the coil of the steam
and

just let

let!

the
emptiness
is

Let

there is so much loss and so much lost on us these days

all i have are thank-yous

(if you're reading this, thank you)

"wash your hands"
but don't wash yourself
so completely that you
clean away every other part
keep room in your pocket
keep room in your heart
for a little dust
just enough trust

and after we have poured out the jars of our anger

and those afraid at the smell and sight rancid old world
mold we forgot is kicking growing below the surface

when we can each and all pay attention look vibrate shake
to the buzz and puss averting sighs

eyes on never off
the unreal glimmer of the lies

some things
come
(at)
unexpected
(times)

the light of the full moon
and fire
flies

we will live to be
fireflies

i
don't
have
any
more
words
just
hands

Notes

All biblical translations are from the JPS Tanakh (2000). All talmudic references are from the Babylonian Talmud.

Part 1

PAGE 21

"The Soul Is Pure," *Service of the Heart: Exploring Prayer*, The Jewish Theological Seminary, last modified April 3, 2013, http://www.jtsa.edu/the-soul-is-pure (see Samuel Barth's teaching about G-d, breath and the grammatical use of the *mappik dot* after the Elohai Neshama prayer)

PAGE 23

Babylonian Talmud, Sanhedrin 37a

Genesis 18:27

PAGE 41

My People's Prayer Book: The Amidah, the Second Edition, p. 85 (see Joel M. Hoffman's translation of 'Selah' in Psalms)

PAGE 44

The Book of Letters, Rabbi Lawrence Kushner (see Rabbi Kushner's teachings on the first two letters of the Hebrew alphabet, aleph and bet. Genesis, the first book of the Hebrew Bible, begins with the second letter of the Hebrew alphabet, bet)

PAGE 102
Psalm 130

Part 2

PAGE 119
Amos 5:24

PAGE 122
Hilchot Kriat Shema, see Chapter 2

PAGE 150
Hallelujah, Leonard Cohen (from the album "Various Positions")

My People's Prayer Book: Shabbat Morning (Shacharit and Musaf), the Tenth Edition, p. 25-26, 36-37 (see Rabbi Lawrence Hoffman's brief note on 'Hallel' in the Psalms and Rabbi Nehemia Landes' historical survey of 'Hallel,' respectively)

"Rashi and the 'Messianic' Psalms." In *Birkat Shalom: Studies in the Bible, Ancient Near Eastern Literature, and Postbiblical Judaism- Presented to Shalom M. Paul on the Occasion of His Seventieth Birthday* (see discussion about the Hebrew word 'Jah' and its etymology)

About the author

Devon Spier is a poet and visual theologian who studies rabbinics at the Academy for Jewish Religion (NY). Online, she uses images on Facebook and Instagram to transmit her existential musings on recovery, pain, multiple identities, hope and belonging.

Her first book of poems, *Heart Map and the Song of Our Ancestors*, was an online poetry bestseller and is currently used as a spiritual storybook by countless individuals and communities of religious difference and dissidence that are reclaiming the paths to their own precious, unique souls across the globe.

Devon has received a Building Women/Building Communities award from the Ontario Government, a Peace Medallion from the YMCA and the Outstanding Achievement Award and Peter C. and Elisabeth Williams Memorial Scholarship from the departments of Religious Studies and Peace and Conflict Studies at the University of Waterloo, respectively.

She has also served as the first Canadian rabbinical student fellow with T'ruah: The Rabbinic Call for Human Rights.